Other Books by Susan Troutt

The Child Pirate

Pirates to the End

The How-to Joke

For Bradley Eric Anderson,
Watch for the clues!! ☺

Susan Troutt
3/21/16

JAKE THE DETECTIVE

Written and Illustrated by

Susan Troutt

authorHOUSE

AuthorHouse™
1663 Liberty Drive
Bloomington, IN 47403
www.authorhouse.com
Phone: 1-800-839-8640

© 2010 Susan Troutt. All rights reserved.

No part of this book may be reproduced, stored in a retrieval system, or transmitted by any means without the written permission of the author.

First published by AuthorHouse 12/21/2010

ISBN: 978-1-4520-6940-1 (sc)
ISBN: 978-1-4520-6941-8 (e)

Printed in the United States of America

Certain stock imagery © Thinkstock.

This book is printed on acid-free paper.

Because of the dynamic nature of the Internet, any Web addresses or links contained in this book may have changed since publication and may no longer be valid. The views expressed in this work are solely those of the author and do not necessarily reflect the views of the publisher, and the publisher hereby disclaims any responsibility for them.

For Patrick, Jack, and Andrew

TABLE OF CONTENTS

Vocabulary Lesson 1
Suspects 7
Treats 11
A Trap 16
Down and Dirty 20
Two Towels, Two Bobble Heads 27
Take Two 32
Yes, Sir! 38
Ants! 43
Catching Angela 47
Following Orders 52
Inside Job 57
Dancing Dust Bunnies 62
Was There Homework? 67
Finding Out 71
The Undercover Mission 76
What's Important 79

VOCABULARY LESSON

Jake couldn't believe it. This was the third time this week that something was missing from his desk. Monday his pencil was missing, and yesterday and again today it was his lunch money.

He peered into his desk slot.

"Jake," said his teacher Miss Winters, "are you paying attention?"

Jake sat up straight. What had Miss Winters been saying? He hadn't realized that she was even talking at all. "Were you saying something?"

"Yes, Jake, we were discussing vocabulary. Please listen."

Jake nodded. His dark hair stuck up at all angles. He tried to smooth it down. It bounced back up again. It was bad enough that he was the smallest kid in his fourth grade class. Why did he have to put up with bad hair too?

His mind began to wander. Who could have taken his things? Mikey had a pencil that looked like his. So did Callie. So did Angela. His pencil had been an ordinary yellow one. There was nothing special about his pencil, except that it was missing. Does *missing* make a pencil special? It was all so confusing.

Just yesterday, his mother had told him to *add* something to the grocery list. Well, anyone who's been in school knows that a list is for spelling words, and that adding is what you do in math. Why didn't his mother understand that?

Jake waved his hand in the air, hoping Miss Winters would stop talking so he could tell her about his missing money.

Finally she came to his desk. "What is it, Jake? Do you need help with your vocabulary words?"

He shook his head.

"Better get to work."

Jake rummaged through his desk. He pulled out a clean sheet of paper. "Miss Winters," he began.

"Yes?"

"Um, my lunch money is missing. It was missing yesterday too."

"Have you looked in your desk?"

"Yes. It's not there."

Miss Winters reached in her pocket. She took out a crisp new dollar bill. "I'll loan you the money, but keep an eye on it."

Keep an eye on it? Jake knew exactly what that meant. The word **on** had been in last week's vocabulary. Miss Winters had told the class that **on** meant **atop**.

Well, he knew what **a top** was. It was a toy that spun round and round. **On** was not a toy top. **On** meant to be **on top of** something. That's what it meant.

Miss Winters was old. Maybe she was confused. *When she told me to keep an eye on this dollar, I'll bet she meant I should put my eye **on top** of it.*

Jake spread the dollar out and placed it on his desk. Slowly he turned his head to the side and eased it downward. He put his eye right on top of the dollar bill. He tried to see the white board. All he could see was a very up close view of his desk.

"Jake," said Miss Winters, "please take your head off the desk."

Oh, boy! thought Jake. *She's giving me a challenge! She wants me to keep my eye on the dollar and take my head off the desk at the same time! I may be the youngest kid in fourth grade, but I'm up for a good challenge any day!*

Jake lifted his head. He scooped up the dollar and pushed it against his eye. He turned his head to the side so his eye was on top of the dollar. Copying words was hard, but a challenge was a challenge.

Pretty soon his neck stiffened and began to ache. He had no idea a challenge could hurt this much. *I can't give up. I've got to keep working so Miss Winters will be proud of me.*

Finally it was lunchtime. The class lined up. Jake stood in line with his head twisted sideways. He couldn't see where he was going, but his eye was still on the dollar.

He followed Mikey, the kid in front of him, to the cafeteria.

He reached for his tray with one hand while the other pressed the dollar to his eye. The tray was heavy—and wobbly.

"Oh, boy!" he said when his milk carton crashed on its side. Jiggling right behind came jittery lime Jell-o.

"Tilt the tray the other way," said Mikey.

Then his fork, as if it had a mind of its own, flipped to the floor.

Jake stopped. He held steady. Dollar to his eye, he felt the floor for his fork.

Mikey came to the rescue. He took the tray and set it down.

"Thanks, Mikey. You're the best," said Jake.

Mikey smiled. "No problem."

"One dollar," said the cashier.

Jake pealed the money from his eye. He offered it to the cashier. "Here's my dollar."

The cashier looked at the sweaty money. "Why is it so wet?"

"Miss Winters gave me a challenge. It was really hard, especially for a nine-year old." Jake seemed very pleased with himself.

The cashier narrowed her eyes at Jake. Then she sighed and put the money in the cash drawer.

SUSPECTS

When Jake came home from school, cousin Clyde was in the living room reading a mystery book. Clyde was always reading. He said it helped him think up new ideas.

Thirteen-year-old Clyde had a pudgy belly and thin hair. His glasses reflected light and made it look as if he had two huge, shiny eyes. But he was filled with great ideas.

Jake liked sharing his day with Clyde. "Guess what! I looked in my desk today, and I couldn't believe it!"

"What?"

"My lunch money was missing. I searched all over. I even took out my books and looked in the back of my desk. What happened to it? It's a mystery—a big mystery. I need to do some detective work."

Clyde looked up. "What did you do about lunch?"

"Miss Winters loaned me the money. She told me to keep an eye on it. I was really good at that. I kept my eye on it all morning long."

Clyde raised an eyebrow. "What about suspects?"

"What are suspects?"

"People you think might have taken it."

"Angela!" shouted Jake. He liked Angela. She was the biggest kid in fourth grade, and she was really smart. "Angela could have done it. She does everything. She's a very good helper."

"So Angela took your lunch money?"

"Well, she's smart. She probably thought she wouldn't get caught."

"Angela. Right?"

"No, wait! Not Angela! She's pretty honest. She wouldn't take anything."

"So not Angela?"

"She's smart," Jake reasoned, "but taking money wouldn't be a very smart thing to do. I guess I don't know who did it."

Cousin Clyde nodded. "Well, treat everyone as if they're a suspect."

"Okay."

"Whoever took the money would have to have a motive."

"What's a motive?"

"It's the reason why someone would commit a crime. Who sits next to you?"

"Robert."

"Robert sits next to you? That would give him the *opportunity* to take your money."

"But Robert is my best friend," protested Jake. "He's ten years old. He has curly black hair. Why would he take my lunch money?"

Clyde shrugged. "You never know what the motive might be."

Now Jake was really puzzled. His mind was everywhere all at once. Who were the suspects? Angela, Robert, Cindy. Mikey, Brandy, Callie, George. Teddy, Lena, Randall.

"Randall! He's always losing things. Maybe Randall lost his own lunch money and needed some. Maybe Randall took my lunch money. George probably didn't do it. George is rich. He doesn't need any more money. But then again, it might be Angela, because she's smart. I hope it isn't Robert."

"Keep thinking," said Clyde. He returned to his reading.

Jake slouched on the couch. He thought about what Clyde had said. *I'm supposed to treat the suspects. Hmmm, I wonder what kind of treats they would like.*

TREATS

The next day Jake brought a bag of candy treats to school. As he passed them out he pretended he was a detective and searched for suspects.

He put a candy on Randall's desk. "Here's one for you, Randall," he said. He watched out the corner of his eye to see if freckle-faced Randall did anything strange.

"Thank you, Jake," said Randall as he opened his candy.

Hmmm, thought Jake. *He has nice manners. He's probably not a thief.*

"One for you, Cindy."

Brown-eyed Cindy, with her straight brown hair, liked Jake. She smiled at him.

He folded his arms and leaned in toward her. "So how's your lunch money, hmmm?"

"What?"

"Do you have lunch money?" Jake repeated.

"Why, yes, I do. Thank you for asking."

So Cindy didn't take my lunch money because she has money of her own, thought Jake. *Who could have taken it?*

He looked around.

There was Brandy. She was really cute.

Jake sighed. He leaned his elbows on Brandy's desk. He stared into her big blue eyes.

"What do you want, Jake?" asked Brandy, flipping her light brown twin pony tails.

"Want?" he asked dreamily.

"Yes, Jake. You're on my desk."

"Oh," Jake said, coming to his senses. "Would you like a candy, Brandy?" He placed one on her desk.

"Hey, that rhymes!" shouted Callie. "Candy-Brandy!"

Jake looked over at Callie, all giggly and silly. She had really long hair that went half way down her back. He handed her a treat.

"Is it your birthday?" she asked. Her voice was loud, just like it always was.

"It's not his birthday, silly," shrieked Lena, another loudmouth. Lena's hair was cut short. Sometimes people asked if she was a girl or a boy. "Jake's birthday was last month. He brought cupcakes, remember?"

"Oh, that's right," agreed Callie. "So what's the occasion?" Callie always wanted to know what was going on.

Jake's smile was twisted. "I'm treating you..." Under his breath he said, "Like suspects."

Suddenly Robert shouted, "Hey! My lunch money is missing!"

Jake spun around.

Robert looked different. His beautiful dark curls were gone. His hair was cropped close to his head. "Robert! What happened to your hair?"

"What do you mean my hair? What happened to my lunch money?"

"What did happen to it?"

"I don't know. It's gone! That's what!"

"Are you sure?" asked Jake.

"Yes," wailed Robert. "Get in my desk. Look for yourself."

Jake stooped down and tried to squeeze his head inside Robert's desk. His head was too big.

At least I know Robert isn't the thief, he thought. *A thief wouldn't steal his own lunch money.*

Robert was still worried. "What am I going to do?"

"Go ask Miss Winters. She'll loan it to you."

Jake watched Miss Winters take out her purse. She handed Robert some money.

When Robert came back to his seat, Jake said, "You'd better keep an eye on that."

"That's what Miss Winters said. That's why I put it right here." Robert patted his back pocket.

Jake frowned. "How can you keep an eye on something in your back pocket?" he asked searching through Robert's hair. "Are there eyes in the back of your head?"

A TRAP

Clyde was good at explaining things, much better than a grownup. He had great ideas and he was really fun to be around.

"My detective work isn't going so well. Do you know any other ways to solve a mystery?" Jake asked later that afternoon.

Clyde looked up from his mystery book. His eyes were huge behind his glasses. "In detective books they set a trap. You could set a trap and catch the thief red-handed."

"That's a great idea!"

Jake was good at following directions. What he wasn't good at was listening. His mind wandered too much.

In math class when Miss Winters taught addition, Jake daydreamed about things he could add together, like adding all the dogs in the neighborhood.

Let's see, Mikey has two dogs, Callie has two, and George has three. How many does that make altogether? Two plus two plus three is—wait, isn't one of George's dogs a cat? Could I add a cat in too?

"Jake," said Miss Winters, "what's the answer to the problem on the board?"

"Do I count cats?" Jake blurted out.

The other students laughed. Jake always said such funny things.

Miss Winters sighed. "Jake, we're not counting cats. We're adding three digit numbers. Please pay attention."

"Yes, Miss Winters," replied Jake. *Pay attention. Pay attention. Pay attention.* He casually slipped his hand into his desk. *Pay attention. Pay attention.* His lunch money was still there. *What's a good way to catch a thief?*

Then he remembered Clyde's idea.

Pretty soon the chance came to make good on Clyde's advice.

Miss Winters was teaching about nouns. "A noun is the name of a person, place, or thing. Jake, can you name a noun for us?"

Jake hopped up on his chair. "A trap!" he

shouted. He shielded his eyes with his hand and spun around to look at his classmates' hands.

"Jake! We do not stand on chairs! Come down from there!" scolded Miss Winters.

Jake frowned. Things weren't going the way they were supposed to. He'd have to try again.

"A trap!" he said loudly and quickly scanned the class. He looked harder this time. Did anyone have red hands?

Miss Winters frowned. "Jake, please sit down."

"A trap!" Jake said, this time from his seat.

Miss Winters sighed. "Yes, Jake, **trap** is a noun."

Jake didn't understand. He'd done exactly what Clyde had told him. He'd said, "A trap," but he didn't catch a thief with red hands. All the kids in his class had normal-colored hands. "I guess none of my classmates are red-handed after all," he mumbled.

For the rest of the class period, Jake sat quietly in his seat. He forgot to pay attention to the noun lesson. He just kept thinking about what Clyde had said. "Say, 'A trap' and catch the thief red-handed." What had he done wrong?

DOWN AND DIRTY

Jake flopped beside Clyde on the couch. "Your advice didn't work. I need another idea to solve this big mystery."

"Still haven't caught the thief, huh?" asked Clyde.

"No, and what's worse, Robert's lunch money is missing too."

"Well, the thief could be anyone. Looks like you'll have to go undercover."

Jake leaped up. "Undercover! Then I've got to start packing!"

He ran to his room and snatched the fuzzy white blanket from his bed. He crammed it into his book bag.

At school the next morning, Callie shouted, "Hey! My quarter is missing. Someone stole my quarter!"

Lena looked in her desk. "My quarter is gone too!"

"Hey! We don't like this. We don't like this one bit," shouted Callie.

Lena put her fists on her hips and made her eyes real big. "Yeah, we were going to buy new pencils at the bookstore this afternoon. Now our money is gone."

"Now, girls," soothed Miss Winters.

"Well, we're just letting you know we don't like that our money is has been stolen," said Callie.

"Yes, yes. I understand." Miss Winters waited for the girls to settle down. Then she looked sadly about the room. "Boys and girls, I have something to tell you."

Everyone wanted to know what was wrong.

She gave the class an unhappy look. "At the beginning of the school year, our classroom had enough supplies for every student in the class. Yesterday when we worked on vocabulary words, there weren't enough dictionaries to go around. Lena and Callie had to share."

"Yeah, and we didn't like that one bit!" loudmouth Lena shrieked.

Miss Winters held a finger to her lips, signaling

Lena to be quiet. Miss Winters waited. Then she said. "I checked the supplies and several other things are missing too. That means that someone has taken things from our classroom. If that someone is in this class, it means we have a thief among us."

The students gasped. Then everyone started whispering about the terrible thing Miss Winters had said. Their voices grew louder and louder until they sounded like a hive of bees.

"Boys and girls!" warned Miss Winters.

George raised his hand. "Who do you think it is?"

Miss Winters looked down at her sensible shoes. She looked up again. She shook her head. "I don't know, George, but I hope that whoever took the supplies will return them and clear his or her name."

How do you clear a name? Jake wondered. He thought about it for a while. Then he came up with the answer. Someone writes your name on the board and erases it. If a person erases his own name, that person is the thief.

Jake decided to watch to see who erased names from the whiteboard.

When recess time came, Jake put the blanket over his head.

"What's the blanket for?" asked Robert.

"I'm going undercover to catch the thief."

"I want to go undercover too," said Robert. "Let me under there with you."

Both boys stuck their heads under the blanket and walked around the playground.

"I can't see where I'm going," complained Robert.

"Just stick with me. I know what I'm doing," said Jake, bumping into something. "Oh, excuse me, Miss Winters. I didn't see you there."

Robert yanked the blanket from his head. "Jake, that wasn't Miss Winters! That was a tree!"

"I can't see very well."

"It's because of this blanket. What if we put it over our heads, but kept our faces out?"

"Yeah!" said Jake. "We'd still be undercover, but then we could see where we were going."

Jake and Robert spread the blanket wide and ducked underneath. Each poked his head out and clutched the blanket beneath his chin. Nothing showed but their faces.

This was a really good idea. They could see

where they were going and watch for suspects too.

"Remember that everyone is a suspect," reminded Jake.

"Right," said Robert.

Jake saw Callie standing alone. "Let's go see about Callie."

Robert looked around. "Where is she?" he asked, starting toward the left.

"She's by the monkey bars," said Jake, starting toward the right.

The boys yanked the blanket in opposite directions. Finally Jake gave a firm tug. Robert toppled over, right on top of him.

"Look at Jake and Robert!" hollered Callie. "They are so funny!"

Everyone came running to see how funny the boys under the blanket looked. Arms and legs in the air, rolling, tossing, squirming, they looked like a giant ghost.

"A monster! A monster!" screamed Lena.

Cindy said, "I'm afraid of monsters. They're scary."

After much twisting and wallowing on the ground, the boys tumbled into a mud puddle.

"Yuck!" hollered Robert. "Now see what you've done!" He pulled free from the blanket. It was quite muddy now, but not as muddy as his pants.

Jake, fighting the blanket, flung his arms

every which way. "Let me out! Let me out!" he screamed.

Miss Winters came to the rescue. She pulled the blanket off Jake. He thrashed on the ground, kicking his feet, waving his arms. He had his eyes closed.

"Jake, there's nothing wrong with you. Get up."

Jake opened his eyes. His classmates were circled round. All of them stared.

Quickly he hopped to his feet. His face burned with embarrassment. "Oh! Miss Winters! I was just looking for you. What are you doing *here*?" he said, brushing off his pants.

Two Towels, Two Bobble Heads

Jake heard Mom's voice all the way from the laundry room. "Jake! Come here!"

He rushed in to find her holding his dirty blanket.

"What, young man, happened to this?"

Jake hung his head. "I used it to go undercover."

"You did more than go under the covers. This blanket is filthy! Did you have your shoes on in bed?"

"No, Mom, I . . ."

Mom shook her head. "You must have had your shoes on. There's muddy footprints all over this blanket!"

Jake shrugged. "I accidentally stepped on it."

"Well, next time take your shoes off before you crawl under the blanket."

Jake's mouth dropped open. Take his shoes off? He hadn't thought of that. That'd be much quieter. If he took his shoes off, he could sneak up on suspects.

"Great idea, Mom! Thanks!"

The corners of Mom's mouth turned up in a smile. "Thank you for being so cooperative."

Jake decided not to take the blanket to school again. He needed something smaller. He looked in the linen closet. "Mom, can I have two beach towels to take to school?"

"Sure, Jake. Take old ones."

Jake pulled two towels from the closet. He crammed them into his book bag.

At school he gave one of the towels to Robert. "These are our new undercover suits."

Robert unfolded his. He held it up. "Cool. Mine says Myrtle Beach. What does yours say?"

Jake pulled back the fold on his. "Virginia Beach." He slipped the towel over his head.

Robert did the same.

"Keep an eye out for the thief," reminded Jake.

On the whiteboard Miss Winters wrote the spelling list. "Copy your words, boys and girls, while I check your papers."

Jake and Robert sat there, heads covered by the beach towels, copying their spelling words. Between letters, they looked around and then wrote another letter.

"What's the next word?" asked Jake.

"Echo."

Both boys wrote E.

Both boys looked right.

Both boys wrote C.

Both boys looked left.

Both boys wrote H.

Both boys looked right.

Both boys wrote O.

Both boys looked left.

"Hey!" shouted Lena. "Jake and Robert look like bobble heads!"

The whole class looked at Jake and Robert. Everyone started to laugh.

"What's going on?" asked Miss Winters.

"Jake and Robert are bobble-head ghosts!" squealed Callie.

Miss Winters stood up. She walked slowly

toward the boys. Everyone waited to see what would happen.

She looked down at Jake and Robert. "The towels are distracting. Put them away please."

The boys drug the towels from their heads. They stuffed them into their table desks.

"Is that it?" screeched Lena. "Is that all there is?" She felt disappointed that things ended so easily.

"Yes, Lena. That's all there is," replied Miss Winters.

Jake leaned over to Robert and whispered in the tiniest of voices, "Maybe next time we should take off our shoes."

TAKE TWO

"Today we are going to make a map of the United States," said Miss Winters. "Angela, would you be a good helper and pass out scissors?"

Angela was always a good helper. She liked to think that she was Miss Winters' best helper. "Yes, Miss Winters," she said, flipping her dark curls.

She rose from her seat and headed toward the supply shelf. She held the scissor rack by the handle. She smiled as she gave each person a pair of scissors. "One for you, Jake, and one for you, Robert. One for you, Callie, and one for you, George."

On her own desk, she put two pair of scissors. Then she continued around the room. "One for you, Randall, and one for you, Lena."

"Did you see that?" Jake whispered to Robert. "She gave herself two pair of scissors."

"So?" said Robert.

"It's mighty suspicious, that's all. What does she need with *two* pair of scissors?"

Jake decided to watch Angela. He stared at her until Miss Winters said, "Jake, don't forget to cut out your map."

"Yes, Miss Winters." Jake picked up his scissors, but he didn't look away from Angela.

Miss Winters asked Angela to pass out glue.

Jake continued to watch. Angela gave everybody one bottle of glue, but side by side on her own desk, she placed two glue bottles.

"That's really suspicious!" Jake whispered.

Robert said, "You're going to get in trouble if you don't cut out your map."

Jake picked up his paper and wedged the scissors along the black line. His eyes never strayed from Angela.

"Now, class," instructed Miss Winters, "glue your map onto construction paper."

Robert did as he was told.

While watching Angela, Jake reached for his map. He turned it over, smeared glue on the back, and stuck it onto blue construction paper.

"Be sure to write your name on your work," directed Miss Winters.

Still looking at Angela, he picked up his pencil and scrawled his name across the paper. He wrote **J A K**, but the **E** ran off onto his desk.

"Angela, would you collect supplies?" asked Miss Winters.

Angela walked around the room with the scissors rack. Clink! Clink! Pairs of scissors dropped into the rack.

When Angela came to her own desk, she picked up a pair of scissors and put it in the rack. George and Teddy put scissors in the rack. Cindy, who shared a table desk with her, put a pair of scissors in the rack too. Everyone else did the same.

Then Angela collected glue bottles. At her own desk, she put one bottle in the box. Cindy put a bottle in the box. Callie put a bottle in the box too. So did everyone else.

"Did you see that?" whispered Jake.

"I did," replied Robert. "She took two scissors and two glues, but only returned one of each!"

"I've solved the mystery!" said Jake. "Angela is the thief!"

Miss Winters asked Angela to pick up everyone's work.

Around the room Angela collected maps. At Jake's desk she stopped and drew in her breath.

Jake narrowed his eyes. "What's the problem, Angela?" In his head he was thinking, *You're a thief! That's the problem!*

Angela burst out laughing.

"What's so funny, Angela?" he snapped.

Angela put her hands on her hips. "You didn't do it right, that's what. Look at your map, Jake."

Jake looked down at his map. It was pasted wrong. Half of it hung off the blue construction paper. But the worst part was the way he'd cut it out. He's lopped off Maine. He'd chopped off Florida. Part of the east coast was missing. What was left of Washington was a triangle, and the southern tip of Texas was nowhere to be found.

Angela pointed at Jake's map and laughed. "You made the United States look like a circle."

Jake looked in the direction of Angela's finger. What she said was true. His United States did indeed look like a circle.

"Miss Winters, Jake didn't do his map activity right!" tattled Angela.

Jake glared at her. *She's trying to distract us so she won't get caught!*

"Never mind, Angela," said Miss Winters. "Have all the students put their supplies away? We're still missing a pair of scissors and a bottle of glue."

Jake raised his hand to tell Miss Winters that Angela had stolen them.

Right then three loud bleeps sounded into the room. There was a pause. Then they started over again.

"Fire drill!" shouted Miss Winters. "Line up! Hands over your mouths, please."

"Miss Winters . . ." began Jake.

"No talking. Hand over your mouth, please Jake. File out of the room, boys and girls. Quickly."

Jake sighed and followed the others out.

YES, SIR!

After school the boys met up with Clyde. Jake was so excited he could scarcely contain himself. "We've been really good detectives. We've solved the big mystery. Now what do we do about the thief?"

Clyde thought he would have a little fun. "I'll help you, but I'm going to be in charge. Is that all right?"

"I guess," said Robert.

"No," said Clyde. "I'm the boss, see? When I tell you what to do, you're supposed to say, 'Yes, sir'. Is that clear?"

"I guess so," shrugged Robert.

"Say, 'Yes, sir!'," Clyde reminded him.

"Yes, sir!" repeated Robert.

"And how about you, Jake?" asked Clyde.

"It's okay with me."

Clyde frowned. "You're supposed to say, 'Yes, sir,' Jake."

"Yes, sir, Jake? That doesn't make sense. Why would I call you Jake? *I'm* Jake," said Jake.

Clyde sighed. "No, Jake, I want you to say, 'Yes, sir!' Got it?"

"Yes, sir."

"I can't hear you," Clyde said in a louder voice.

"Why can't you hear me?" asked Jake. "I said it plenty loud."

"Just say, 'Yes, sir!'"

"Okay," said Jake, shrugging his shoulders.

This wasn't the way it was supposed to go. Clyde leaned toward Jake. His face did not look happy. "Jake!"

"What?"

"Just do what I tell you. Say, 'Yes, sir!'"

"Oh, I get it," smiled Jake. "This is a game! Okay. Yes, sir!"

"Line up," ordered Clyde.

Jake and Robert hurried to stand one in front of the other, just like they did in Miss Winters' class.

Clyde folded his hands behind his back. His shirt gapped a little in front. He pulled it together. Like a drill sergeant he paced back and forth in front of the boys. "From now on you will follow my orders. Do you hear?"

"We hear you, Clyde," said Jake. "We're standing right in front of you. Aren't we, Robert?"

"Yes, sir!" Robert replied with feeling.

"I want this to be clear. That's why I 'm speaking loudly," said Clyde. "Got that?"

The boys grinned. "Yes, sir!"

Clyde drew in closer. "Now, tell me. Who's the suspect?"

Jake answered immediately. "Angela! During map class, she took two pair of scissors."

"And two glue bottles," reminded Robert.

Clyde raised an eyebrow. "So?"

"So everyone knows you're only supposed to take one."

"And she only put back one of each," said Jake.

"Hmmm," said Clyde. "Sounds suspicious all right! Better put a tail on her."

The boys' eyes lit up. "Yes, sir!"

"And don't forget to act like gentlemen," reminded Clyde.

"Yes, sir!" Jake and Robert could hardly wait to get started.

"I'll get cardboard and scissors and crayons. You get tape," suggested Jake.

The boys ran off in opposite directions.

By the time Robert returned, Jake's face was red with excitement. "This is going to be good!" he told Robert.

On the paper, he drew a long tiger tail. He colored it orange and black. He cut it out. He held it up for approval. "What do you think?"

"Looks grrrreat!" replied Robert.

ANTS!

"I'll bring the tiger tail. You bring the tape," Jake told Robert.

He pulled his beach towel inside-out over his head. "Put on your undercover suit."

"Okay," said Robert, pulling the white side of his towel over his head too.

With their heads covered, the boys looked like a pair of ghosts walking down the street.

They looked both ways and sure enough, along came Angela.

"Lay low," whispered Robert.

Jake threw himself face first, arms out straight, flat against the ground. "Like this?"

Robert looked down at Jake. "I. . .I guess so," he said uncertainly. "You look pretty silly lying there. How can you see what's going on?"

Jake lifted his head. "It's not laying low if my head is up."

Robert didn't answer.

Jake decided to turn his head to the side. That would have to do.

Robert ducked behind a big oak tree. "Here she comes!"

"Where?" Jake couldn't see Angela. He couldn't see anything except the ground.

"Right there! Look!"

Jake opened his eyes real wide. Blades of grass twitched in front of his nose. An ant crawled over a twig. Jake squirmed as it went up one side and down the other. Jake didn't like bugs.

"Shhh!" warned Robert. "Lie still or she'll see you."

Jake felt something creeping up his leg. He twisted in that direction. It was an ant. Then he saw another ant and another. There were ants everywhere! He was lying on an ant hill!

As if he were catapulted by a slingshot, Jake leaped off the ground. Clutching his towel under his chin, he ran in circles screaming, "Help! Help! Ants! Ants!"

Robert was speechless. He couldn't believe Jake was acting this way.

Jake ran around and around the oak tree, waving his arms. His towel flapped like white bat wings. "Ants! Ants!" he shrieked. His high pitched voice sounded like a little girl's.

"Jake," hissed Robert. "What are you doing?"

"Help me, Robert! Help me! Ants are crawling all over me!"

Robert ripped the beach towel away from Jake. "There. The ants are gone! See?" He shook the towel up and down a few times. "Gone!"

Jake stopped running. He sucked in his breath. He ran his hand over his arm.

Robert scowled. "Angela's gone too."

Jake looked around. Robert was right. Angela was nowhere in sight. He felt foolish for the way he'd acted. He reached for the towel. "Then we'll just have to go undercover again."

Robert sighed and pulled his towel over his head too.

This time, the towels were right-side-out. The words **Virginia Beach** and **Myrtle Beach** were scrawled across their backs. Down the sidewalk they walked, looking just like ghosts on a beach vacation.

CATCHING ANGELA

Pretty soon Angela walked back in their direction.

The boys ducked behind a tree.

She was chanting some sort of jump rope rhyme.

"Down in the valley where the green grass grows,

There sat Callie as sweet as a rose.

She sang, she sang, she sang so sweet,

Along came Teddy and kissed her on the cheek.

How many kisses did she get?"

"Oh, poor Teddy," Jake whispered to Robert. "He has to kiss Callie!"

"Shhh! She'll hear you," said Robert. He leaned out from the tree to get a better look. "Pip

pip, old chap. I do believe she has passed us by. Let us hurry onward."

Jake's eyebrows went up. "Why are you talking like that?"

"I'm acting like an English gentleman," said Robert.

"Huh?"

"Clyde said to act like gentlemen."

"Oh! I get it! Okay, I'll act like an old gentleman!" Jake's words came from the side of his mouth. "How's this?" he asked in a raspy voice.

Robert laughed.

"Shhh, she'll hear us," Jake said out of the side of his mouth.

They darted to the next tree, heads covered, towel ends flying in the wind.

"Watch her," rasped Jake's side-mouth voice.

"Right-o, old chap."

Robert dashed to the next tree. Jake was right behind.

This was really fun! Both boys clamped hands over their mouths to keep from laughing out loud. Laughs escaped anyway. They sounded like squeaky little dog toys.

When the boys looked, Angela was gone.

Jake forgot to talk from the side of his mouth. "Hey! Where'd she go?"

He pulled his towel tighter over his head.

Robert did the same.

They looked right. They looked left. They

looked right. They looked left. They did not see Angela.

But Angela saw them. She was right behind them. In her softest voice she whispered, "Where do you think she went?"

"I don't know," said Jake. "She was right here, but now she's gone."

"Why don't you look behind you," whispered Angela.

"Why don't *you* look behind *you*," retorted Robert, irritated at Jake for being so bossy.

Jake turned around. The towel was over his head. He did not see Angela.

She stepped beside him.

Jake said, "She's not there."

"Look behind you," whispered Angela.

"I just did. She wasn't there," insisted Jake.

"What's wrong with you?" said Robert.

"Me? What's wrong with *you*?"

Robert held up a fist. "Are you looking for a fight?"

"No, but you are!" shouted Jake, also raising his fist.

Robert's face twisted into a sneer.

Jake's did the same.

This was Angela's big chance. "Well, if it isn't the Beach Sisters!"

"Huh?" said Jake, spinning around.

"Beach Sisters?" said Robert.

"Yes, Beach Sisters," repeated Angela. "Myrtle and Virginia Beach! That's what it says on your towels."

"We're not sisters," said Jake.

Robert didn't know what to say.

Then Jake came to his senses. He yanked the towel off his head and tossed it over Angela's. "Get her!" he yelled.

FOLLOWING ORDERS

Robert threw his towel over Angela's head too. He twisted the ends into a knot. "Put the tail on her!" he shouted.

Angela was a lot taller than Robert. She kept wiggling around. He could barely hold on.

"Mmmmm!" came Angela's muffled voice.

Jake tore off a big piece of tape. It stuck to his fingers.

"Mmmmm! Mmmmm!" grunted Angela. She was all arms and legs, squirming, kicking, toppling over.

Jake twisted the tape from one finger to another. "How am I going to get this sticky stuff off my hands? Look, it's on my hand." Jake touched his fingers to the tape on his right hand. "Hey! Now it's on my left hand. Wherever I touch, the tape sticks, see?" He moved the tape from one hand to the other.

"Jake, hurry!" Robert begged. He snatched the tiger tail from Jake's pocket and pressed it against Angela's pants. "Tear off another piece of tape!"

Jake held up his hands. "Look, the tape's on my right hand. Now it's on my left. Now right. Now. . ."

"Jake!"

"What?"

"Some tape, please?"

"Tape? Oh, you want tape. Okay. Why didn't you say so?" Jake balanced the dispenser between his wrists. With his teeth, he snared the tape end. He pulled hard. A long piece broke off. He pressed it clumsily over the tail.

Angela bucked up and down. She was all over the place. It was like taping a tail on a wild donkey.

Then Clyde showed up. In the blink of an eye, before anyone knew what was happening, he had each boy by an arm. "What do you think you're doing?"

"Following orders, sir," said Jake proudly. He pointed to the orange and black striped thing they'd taped crookedly to Angela's pants. "We put a tail on her."

A choking sound came from beneath the towel. Clyde yanked the towel away. There was Angela. Her dark curly hair hung limply around her face.

"What did you do?" she shrieked, trying to see her back side. "You put a tail on me?"

"Yes, and we caught a thief," retorted Jake. "Just like Clyde said we would."

"A thief? Are you calling me a thief?"

"Yes. Thief!"

"Well, you're a—a knucklehead!"

"Well, you're a THIEF!"

"KNUCKLEHEAD!"

"THIEF!"

Clyde stepped between them. "Wait a minute. Why do you think Angela's a thief?"

"She took two pair of scissors," said Jake.

"And she only returned one," reminded Robert.

"And she took two bottles of glue," said Jake.

"And she only returned one," Robert chimed in.

Angela's face turned angry red. "I didn't take two of anything!"

"Yes, you did," Jake responded promptly. "Yes. We saw you put two scissors and two glues on your desk."

"Two? One was for Cindy. Did you forget she's my desk partner?"

"But we saw you put only one away," recalled Robert.

Angela put her hands on her hips. "That's because Cindy put away her own supplies."

Jake looked at Robert. Robert looked at Jake. "Oh," they said at the same time.

"I did see Cindy put supplies away," murmured Robert.

"Yeah, me too," admitted Jake.

The boys hung their heads.

Clyde nodded. "Well, boys, have something to tell Angela?"

"I guess you aren't a thief," mumbled Jake.

Angela ripped off the tiger tail and hurled it at Jake. "I should say not!"

"I'm sorry for thinking you were," said Jake.

"Me too," said Robert.

Angela was still angry. She flicked her limp, dark curls off her shoulders. Her eyes flashed with fire.

Jake patted down his hair uncertainly. "Are we still friends?"

Angela stared at him, at the stupid tiger tail. He was just a silly boy. "Okay. But it better not happen again."

INSIDE JOB

"Clyde," moaned Jake, "I'm the detective, but I need help to solve this mystery."

"Okay," said Clyde. "I'll give you a few more tips."

He went to the closet and came back wearing a black cape and a tall black hat. In front of Jake's face, he fanned a deck of cards. "Ladies and Gentlemen! You are about to see the most amazing magic trick in the whole wide world!" He leaned toward Jake. "Pick a card, any card.

Jake drew one from the stack. "It's a three of hearts."

"You're not supposed to tell what it is!"

"Why not?"

"I'm supposed to guess what card you picked."

"But I already told you what card I picked."

"That's not the way it works!"

"What do you mean?"

Clyde mysteriously rippled his black cape. "Solving a mystery is like doing magic. Magicians distract their audience so they can make their move when no one's looking. It's the same with solving mysteries. You have to be fast. You have to be quick. You have to be smart."

"Huh?"

"Suspect everyone. When you think you have the right guy, follow him. Don't take your eyes off him for a minute."

"Okay. Then what?"

Clyde wiggled his fingers around Jake's ears. "Watch carefully, Ladies and Gentlemen. Ta-da!" Between his fingers, as if he had pulled it out of thin air, was a quarter. He held it out to Jake.

"Hey! How did you do that?" Jake exclaimed.

"It's like I said. Watch your suspects carefully."

"But how will I figure out who's taking things if there aren't any suspects?"

Clyde thought for a moment. "Dust for fingerprints! That's a good way to catch someone with sticky fingers."

Jake's face clouded. *Where am I going to find enough dust for that?* Then an idea came to him. He broke into a big smile. "Oh, I get it! Thanks, Clyde! You're the best!"

School was closed for the day. Outside the building, Jake covered his head with the Myrtle Beach towel. On tiptoes he rang the doorbell.

Mr. Cobb, the custodian, opened the door. "School's closed. What do you want?"

"I need something from my classroom," Jake mumbled.

"What? I can't hear you."

"I need something from my classroom."

"Huh? Speak up!"

"Speak up?"

"Yes."

"Okay." Jake crouched down low. "I - need - some - thing - from - my - class - room!" he said. On each word he sprang from the ground like a frog on springs.

Mr. Cobb frowned. "What are you doing?"

"I'm speaking up. That's what you told me to do."

Mr. Cobb's mouth turned down.

Jake felt the need to explain. "I'm little, see? The only way I can speak UP is to jump there."

Mr. Cobb frowned harder. Then his cell phone rang. He turned his back on Jake. "Hello?"

Jake looked around. No one was watching. The door was open. He went inside.

DANCING DUST BUNNIES

In his classroom Jake flicked on the lights. A shiny plastic baggie, sticky with jelly but just right to put dust in, dangled from the side of the wastebasket.

Jake ran his finger along the chalk tray. "This is a pretty good place for dust." He looked at his finger. Strange. There wasn't any dust.

Then he remembered. A few months ago the school replaced chalk boards with whiteboards.

Now where was he going to find dust for fingerprints?

He looked behind the wastebasket, beneath the teacher's desk, beside closets. No dust. Then his eyes fell on the computer. It was always dusty under there.

He was crouched down on his hands and knees, ready to pick up a thick clump of dust, when the air conditioning came on. "Achoo!" he sneezed. "Achoo! Achoo!"

Dust balls flew along the floor like fuzzy, dancing rabbits. *No wonder they call them dust bunnies!* "Here, little bunny! Hop in," he called as he stuffed each one into the jellied baggie.

Suddenly from the hall, he heard Mr. Cobb's voice. "Time to lock up."

Jake hunkered down by the computer.

The door opened. Mr. Cobb appeared. He turned out the lights. He closed the door.

Click!—Jake heard a clacking sound. Mr. Cobb had locked him in!

Jake flew to the door. He jiggled the doorknob. It wouldn't turn. What was he going to do? Miss Winters wouldn't be here until morning.

He ran his hands through his hair, which stuck up like little porcupine quills. "Why do I have to be locked in and have bad hair too?" he moaned, looking out the window.

On the swings was a curly-haired someone. That someone was Angela!

Jake raced to the window. "Angela! Angela!" he called.

She looked around.

"Angela! It's me—Jake!" He grabbed his undercover towel and waved it out the window like a white flag. "Angela! Angela! I need your help!"

Angela saw the waving towel. She rushed over. "What are you doing in there?" she demanded.

"I'm locked in. I can't get out. Please help me."

"Climb through the window."

That seemed simple enough. Jake threw the towel over his head. He pulled the window inward. It opened a few inches. Beyond that, it wouldn't budge.

"Go through the top window," said Angela.

Jake climbed on the sill. He turned the top window's lever. The window tilted outward.

Little Jake's legs were short. He pretended he was an octopus with eight legs. He tried to shimmy up the slick glass. When he reached the top window, he tottered on the window's edge, one leg in, one leg out.

His body titled toward the out leg. "Whoa!" he shouted. He leaned back in. His body swung inward. "Whoa!" he shouted again. He felt as if he were a teeter-totter. No, he was a clock with legs that read 4:45. He looked down—way down.

"Come on," said Angela.

"It's a long way down there!"

Angela shrugged. "Okay. Suit yourself."

"Wait! How will I get down?"

"Jump."

Jake swallowed hard. "Jump?"

"Yes, Jake." She tugged on his leg. "Jump."

"Wait!" He hung on for dear life. "I'm not ready! Give me a minute!"

Angela pulled. He fell into her arms. She set him on the ground. "Well, that was easy."

Jake looked down. "I'm not even hurt!"

"Better shut that window." Angela pushed the high window with a big stick until it closed.

"Angela, you're really smart."

She tossed her dark curls. "I know," she said, walking off.

Jake picked up the towel. It was covered with dead grass. He brushed it off. He looked back through the window.

On the reading table lay the dust-filled baggie. The jelly-coated dust bunnies had already turned a funky shade of purple.

WAS THERE HOMEWORK?

Jake needed dust to dust for fingerprints. He had to get that baggie. That baggie, with droplets of jelly inside, would make it easy to catch someone with sticky fingers.

How could he get back in the classroom? "I'll just climb through the window," he said to himself.

He threw his legs as high as he could. His short legs wouldn't reach anywhere near the window sill.

"I'll use Angela's stick like a rope and pull myself in."

He found the stick on the ground. It was broken, shorter now. Maybe he could hook it onto the window frame.

After several tries, the stick snagged the edge of the window frame.

Jake tugged. The stick slipped. He fell to the ground.

"What am I going to do?" he moaned.

From the hallway beamed a thin ray of light. Mr. Cobb had opened the classroom door. Jake heard him say, "Holler for me when you're finished."

Jake stood on tiptoes and peered in the window. He was surprised by what he saw.

He saw Brandy. His heart did a dance of love.

Brandy carried her blue book bag. She set it on the table.

She removed two dictionaries from the shelf. She stacked them on the table.

She opened the supply cabinet and stood there for a moment, as if trying to make up her mind. Finally she selected red-handled scissors, colored paper, and green pencils, which she put beside the dictionaries.

Jake wondered what she was doing. He didn't have to wonder long.

Brandy picked up the supplies and stuffed them into her bag.

Jake was shocked. "Brandy! What are you doing?"

Brandy didn't hear him.

She hoisted the book bag onto her shoulder.

She walked to the door. She turned out the light. "Mr. Cobb, I'm finished!" she called. She closed the door behind her.

Jake felt weak. He loved Brandy. Why did she put that stuff in her book bag?

Maybe it's for homework. Jake couldn't remember if there was homework tonight or not. "Why didn't I pay attention in class? Maybe Miss Winters assigned something when I wasn't listening. That's probably it! I'll have to ask someone. Who can I ask? Brandy! I'll ask Brandy!"

As fast as he could he raced around outside the school. Maybe he would meet up with Brandy at the front door.

FINDING OUT

Brandy was already on her way down the sidewalk.

"Brandy! Brandy!" he called, or at least that's what he meant to say. He was out of breath. It came out more like, "Braaaaaa! Braaaaaa!"

When he caught up with her, his face was red, his forehead was sweaty. "Braaaaa! Braaaaa!" he panted.

"What do you want, Jake?"

"Braaaaa!" he wheezed. "Braaaaa!"

"I can't understand a thing you're saying."

Jake doubled over. He tried to catch his breath.

Brandy flipped her twin pony tails. She gave him an impatient look.

Jake choked out two words. "B-Brandy. W-Wait."

Brandy folded her arms across her chest. She tapped her foot. "I'm waiting."

Jake gasped a few more times. Finally he squeaked out, "Do we have homework?"

"What? Why would you ask me that?"

It was hard to breathe. Jake squeezed out another breath. "I saw you with your b-books. I thought maybe we had h-homework."

Brandy rolled her eyes. "No, Jake, we do not have homework."

Jake started to say something. Then he stopped. A funny, sinking feeling came over him. "Brandy, if we don't have homework, then why . . .?" He couldn't go on. He loved Brandy. She couldn't be taking those things from the classroom. She couldn't be—he didn't want to say, or even think it—a thief.

"Why what, Jake?"

He had to get it over with, get it all out at once. "Why do you have your book bag?" he blurted.

"To pick up a few things from the classroom."

Jake's heart felt like it was breaking. *Brandy is the thief!*

He glued his eyes to that book bag. "What kind of things," he said, but he already knew the answer.

"My mother is in charge of a charity. It helps needy children in foreign countries. These kids are really poor. They don't even have enough money to buy school supplies. I'm helping my mother collect money and supplies so these poor children can go to school." She seemed very proud of herself.

"School supplies? Is that what's in your book bag?"

"Yes, Jake. I just told you that."

Jake's hands were shaking. He hated saying this. "Those school supplies came from our classroom."

"Yes. Of course. I know that."

"You stole them."

Brandy blinked her eyes. "I did not steal them, Jake. Our classroom has lots of supplies. Those poor children don't have any. I'm sharing what we have."

Jake looked down at the sidewalk. He felt sad. "They aren't yours to share."

Brandy opened her mouth. No words came out. She set her book bag on the pavement.

Jake said it again. "They aren't yours."

Brandy blinked her eyes. In a little voice she said, "I know they aren't mine, but I wanted them to be." Her eyes filled with tears. "I wanted to help the poor children." A sad little teardrop trickled down her cheek.

Jake felt really bad. "Don't cry," he said. "We can make this right."

"We can?"

"We'll go undercover and put everything back." He shook out the beach towel.

"But what about the needy children?"

Jake pulled the towel over his head. "We'll think of a way to help them. It'll be a secret mission. When you're undercover, no one knows who you are. Would you like to go undercover with me?"

Brandy looked at Jake, at his Myrtle Beach beach towel. "I guess so."

Jake held the towel open for her. She ducked underneath.

THE UNDERCOVER MISSION

Brandy had a little red wagon. They loaded it full of the school's things. They didn't cover themselves with the beach towel. This time, it was the school supplies that were undercover.

Brandy pulled the wagon. Jake pushed from behind.

When they got to school, Brandy rang the bell. Mr. Cobb opened the door. He looked at Jake and frowned, but to Brandy he said, "Forget something?"

"Yes," she replied sweetly.

Jake jumped up and down as he said, "We – forgot – our – books."

Brandy gave Jake a puzzled look.

"Mr. Cobb is hard of hearing," he explained. "You have to speak up."

Mr. Cobb rolled his eyes and shook his head. "Don't be long. Holler when you're finished. I'm almost ready to go home."

"Okay!" said Jake. He jumped up in the air once. He'd only said one word. He felt silly.

In the classroom they began to put things back where they belonged.

Brandy looked sad. "You won't give me away, will you, Jake?"

"No."

Brandy put Jake's money inside his desk. She did the same for Robert and the others. "I know what I did was wrong, but I still want to help the needy children."

Jake kept taking things from the wagon and putting them away. When he'd finished, he turned to Brandy. "I know what you could do."

"What?"

"Ask everyone to bring in money or school supplies to donate to the children."

"Oh, Jake! That's a great idea!"

"I know Principal Fuller would approve this. It doesn't have to be just our class. The whole school could pitch in. We'll make posters and put them around, asking everyone to help."

"Jake, you're pretty smart!"

Jake's heart fluttered. Brandy liked his idea!

WHAT'S IMPORTANT

At school Brandy stood in front of the class, explaining about the charity. She held up the posters she and Jake had made. "At the end of the week we'll give everything we collect to my mother's charity. The ladies will box it up and ship it overseas. Then the poor children can go to school, just like we do."

"What a wonderful idea!" said Miss Winters. "Isn't that a good idea, boys and girls?"

Everyone clapped to show that they agreed.

"Students, I have some other good news."

"What? What?" everyone asked.

"Whoever took the school supplies has done the right thing and returned everything."

"Including the money," said Robert, holding up his dollar.

"Who was the thief?" asked Lena.

"Oh," said Miss Winters, "I don't think that's important!"

"It is too important!" shouted Lena. "Our money was stolen. We want to know who took it!"

Miss Winters raised her hand to quiet the class. "What's important is that whoever took it showed great honesty. No harm was done. It was all made right, wouldn't you agree?"

The class clapped again.

"Now let's get back to normal," she said. "How about recess?"

"So early?" shouted Callie.

Miss Winters smiled. "Yes. We're celebrating the return of our supplies."

Everyone cheered and lined up to go outside. Brandy hung back.

She was the last one on the playground. She stood silently beside Miss Winters.

Miss Winters gave her a kind look. "Is something wrong, Brandy?"

Brandy's eyes were filled with tears. "It was me. I was the one who took the things."

"I know, Brandy."

A pink blush came over Brandy's cheeks. "I did it for the charity."

Miss Winters touched her shoulder. "I guessed as much. Thank you for telling me."

"I'll make it right. I promise I will."

Miss Winters smiled kindly. "You already have, Brandy. You already have."

Brandy threw her arms around her teacher. "Thank you, Miss Winters. Thank you for understanding," she said before she ran off to play.

Jake was waiting on the playground. "Brandy!" he called.

Brandy ran right to him. "Thanks for helping me."

Suddenly shy, Jake looked down at his shoes. There was a scuff on one of the toes. *How did that get there?* His mind began to wander. Did it happen when he climbed out the window? Maybe it was when he tried to push the window. *I wonder if Miss Winters ever had a scuff on her shoes.*

Brandy watched him for a little while. Then she said, "Do you want to play on the monkey bars?"

Brandy? Asking him to play? "Sure," he said.

He picked up his beach towel to put over his head. Then he laughed. "The big mystery's already solved. My detective work is done. I guess I don't need this anymore." He tossed the towel away and raced across the playground. Brandy with the twin pony tails and big blue eyes was right behind him.

ABOUT THE AUTHOR

Susan Troutt, who grew up in Louisville, Kentucky, is the author of *The How-to Joke, The Child Pirate,* and *Pirates to the End.* She and her husband now live in Northern Kentucky with a tuxedo cat named Spatz, a border collie named Mattie, and a sheltie named Rylie.

LaVergne, TN USA
08 January 2011
211496LV00001B/1/P